Nathaniel Colgan, 1851–1919

Maynooth Studies in Local History

SERIES EDITOR Michael Potterton

This is one of six volumes in the Maynooth Studies in Local History series for 2022. It is also my first year as series editor, having taken over the role from the irreplaceable Raymond Gillespie, who held that position from 1995 to 2021, overseeing the publication of a veritable treasure trove of studies in those 27 years. Raymond established the series with Irish Academic Press as a direct result of the enormous success of the Maynooth MA in Local History programme, which began in 1992. Under Raymond's supervision, some 153 volumes were produced, authored by 140 different scholars (94 men and 46 women). The first volume, on education in nineteenth-century Meath, was written by Paul Connell, and the 153rd, on the Dublin Cattle Market in the 1950s and 1960s, was by Declan O'Brien. Eleven people have each contributed two volumes to the series, while Terry Dooley is the only person to have written three.

The remarkable collection now covers some 1,500 years of history across 31 counties, dealing variously with aspects of agriculture and fishing, architecture, crime and punishment, death and burial, economy and trade, education, famine, gender, healthcare, industry, language and literature, migration, music and the arts, politics, religion, society, travel and communication, urban development, war and much more besides. I am grateful to Raymond for entrusting the series to me, and to Four Courts Press for not vetoing the appointment. Together, I am sure that we can build on the sound foundations established over more than quarter of a century of diligent work.

The current crop of titles takes us from a broad look at religion and society in medieval Galway to a very specific and tragic event in Knockcroghery village on the night of 20 June 1921. En route we witness the gradual dismantling of Irish lordship in early modern north Co. Cork, and the development of nursing and midwifery in Co. Tipperary at the turn of the twentieth century. Finally, we have biographical sketches of two remarkable men of the nineteenth century – Thomas Conolly (1823–76) of Castletown House in Co. Kildare and botanist Nathaniel Colgan (1851–1919) of Dublin.

While the genesis and home of this series lie firmly at Maynooth, it is a mark of its appeal, its breadth and its inclusivity that this year's contributors are drawn from Carlow College, Glenstal Abbey, NUI Galway, Trinity College Dublin and the University of Limerick as well as Maynooth University.

Maynooth Studies in Local History: Number 154

Nathaniel Colgan, 1851–1919: the life, times and genealogy of an enigmatic Dubliner

John Colgan

FOUR COURTS PRESS

Set in 11.5pt on 13.5pt Bembo by
Carrigboy Typesetting Services for
FOUR COURTS PRESS LTD
7 Malpas Street, Dublin 8, Ireland
www.fourcourtspress.ie
and in North America for
FOUR COURTS PRESS
c/o IPG, 814 N Franklin Street, Chicago, IL 60610

© John Colgan 2022

ISBN 978-1-80151-033-2

Printed in Ireland
by SprintPrint, Dublin

Contents

FIGURES

Acknowledgments

In the 1980s my father presented me with a small file of baptism and marriage certificates compiled by his youngest uncle, Thomas Colgan, a printer. Thomas had become disabled after losing a limb, and he was then living in a Dublin Corporation house in Cabra. Thomas had gathered this material about his own Colgan family who had lived and worked in Clarendon Street, Dublin, for around 120 years. They dated back to about 1812. He was the youngest of twelve children born alive, only six of whom were living at the censuses of 1901 and 1911. My grandfather, John, or John Fidelus on his baptismal certificate, was the eldest of this brood. As a youngster growing up in my family home and immersed in engineering studies and weekend dancing, I never heard much of my Colgan grandparents, who had died before my parents married. My paternal grandparents and family lived in rooms above the first corporation public library in Dublin, at 102 Capel Street, and my mother, similarly, over a brush factory in number 96. My father's father was a tailor who made uniforms; I still don't know where. I regret that the Department of Social Welfare does not publish the employment records of persons; I did get my own from them. I resolved to commence the forensic detective work to learn more of my roots believing that they surely did not always live in Dublin. This took me to the Registry of Deeds where I examined as many of the 'tombstones' and townland books as I thought would include Colgans, for the most part tenants. Those who use the splendid premises on Henrietta Street/Constitution Hill will know that nothing was indexed by tenant, only by landlord, so it is not a straightforward process. I also trawled through the 1950s-vintage microfilmed copies of Roman Catholic parish registers, most of which from Dublin are in the National Library on Kildare Street. While there I casually exchanged small talk with folk from abroad who were spending a few expensive days in Dublin, in a desperate quest to find their Irish roots; these included at least one Colligan woman from Liverpool. Feeling empathy, I resolved to aim to create a database to help all Colgans locate their Irish roots. In the end, I examined about eighty-four rolls of parish microfilms. At the National Archives I examined hard copies of the two published censuses and some 350 Colgan wills and testaments; fortunately, the latter had been indexed by the staff. I also spent spare days and Sundays visiting many graveyards and recorded relevant gravestone inscriptions. The Gilbert Memorial Library at Pearse Street, Dublin, provided on open shelf a run of street directories; other county libraries, such as those at Letterkenny and Portlaoise, have similar local material. The General Register Office in Lombard Street and elsewhere provided access to their registers, and copies at a modest fee. Most of this was garnered long before data became available online, such as the censuses of 1901 and 1911. I later subscribed to British and Irish newspapers online and searched these for Colgan material. From this extensive trawl, I have created a Colgan chronology of close to 2,000 A4 pages; spreadsheet files of around 13,000 births and baptisms and 4,000 marriages; smaller ones on Colgans in the Constabulary and in the National Army Census, 1922, and individual files, including family trees on individual Colgan clans with occasional inputs from relatives.

I wish to acknowledge the support of all the archives' and libraries' staffs who provided assistance in many ways while on this journey. While undertaking this work, I came upon the unusual name of Nathaniel Colgan, doubly unusual for not being a Roman Catholic Colgan; his only married sibling, William, was not only a brilliant Dublin University scholar, but also an Irish-speaking priest of the Church of Ireland. Nathaniel featured in the newspapers for being a naturalist and botanist, conspicuously for his populist work on the shamrock. By chance I got to know Dr Declan Doogue, president of the Dublin Naturalists' Field Club, when we served as members of Kildare County Council's Leixlip Spa Committee for some years, me in my capacity as a representative of Leixlip Tidy Town Association, which aimed to foster the development as a place to visit and, contrary wise, the other interest groups intent on leaving matters as they were! Dr Doogue is an expert on Nathaniel Colgan's work on Co. Dublin's wild plants and led a group which replicated the seminal study done by Nathaniel with a little help from his sisters and brothers. Nathaniel's study, *Flora of the county Dublin*, was published in 1904. The sequel, compiled after fresh field work, edited by some members of the Dublin Naturalists' Field Club, and sharing a similar title, was published in 1998.

I also acknowledge the assistance of local historians in Co. Kildare: those in the Co. Kildare Federation of Local History Groups, the Library service and Dr Seamus Cullen who provided encouragement and information on the Watson ancestors of Nathaniel Colgan, whose father, a pawnbroker, was Nathaniel Watson Colgan. Lastly, I wish to acknowledge the counsel of Dr Michael Potterton, Department of History, Maynooth University, and Series Editor in succession to Prof. Raymond Gillespie, in bringing the final iteration of this monograph to completion.

Introduction

The *Dictionary of Irish biography* which was published by the Royal Irish Academy in 2009 provided a short, and somewhat tentative, section on Dubliner Nathaniel Colgan MRIA. It was unsure of who his parents were. His family background was a mystery. There are reasons for this, which will unfold within these pages. Many of his peers believed his seemingly shy and diffident nature is the reason for this lack of information on his early life, other than his botanical expertise and awareness of his mountaineering adventures. He did have interests outside of the realm for which he became well-known and acclaimed: wild plants, the 'real' shamrock, and his one-man survey of all of Co. Dublin's wild plants, which took him over a decade to bring to publication, *Flora of the County Dublin*, his real work of legacy, at the age of 53. This handbook of the county's wild plants formed the reference work for over ninety years after it was published in 1904. Though his younger brother William did, Nathaniel did not receive a university education. He was an autodidact, learning as he went, and a linguist, the latter, one presumes, with the help of William, who had learnt even more foreign languages in Trinity College Dublin. Both brothers were *Gaeilgeoirí*. Nathaniel's researches extended to finding Irish names for plants after meeting native speakers and assessing the impact of Dublin's Vikings on plant names. After he and his remaining siblings – all unmarried like himself – moved to a grand house overlooking Bullock Harbour, Co. Dublin, and his magnum opus was finished, he turned his attention to researching the marine life of his surroundings. Photography and making slide presentations of his travels abroad were among his other hobbies. He was a member of the Dublin or Metropolitan Photographic Society, and exhibited with them. Almost all of this was done in the run up to the year 1900, the marine work excepted, and without access to modern technology and instant access to plant and marine images. Within the United Kingdom, he showed signs of opposing English claims to plants when they were not warranted. He

1. Nathaniel Colgan, aged about 31 years

was a supporter of home rule, while holding a sensitive public post, his 'day job', at the highest level.

Authored by a chronicler of all who call themselves any version of Colgan, and voluntary administrator of a Colgan DNA project with ftdna.com, this monograph seeks to unravel a little of the mystery surrounding this man who had several strings to his bow. He had a difficult start in life: two younger siblings died within days of each other of scarlatina; he lost one parent at the age of ten, and the second at fourteen. He and his surviving siblings appear to have been raised by or for his grandfather (who outlived all but one of his own large family of children) and he won a position through open competition into the UK's public service at the age of 20 (the UK then including Ireland). He had some say in where he wanted to work and chose a role as clerk in the Dublin police court. There he remained, some would say by choice, too, so that he could pursue his real interests, until he reached retirement age. During his forty-five years there he rose to the dizzy height of chief clerk.

He died of cancer in October 1919, working on papers up to his death – another reading his last presentation on his behalf. With the death of Nathaniel's elder brother, John Joseph Colgan, in January 1920, the male family line of five generations died out.

1. A tragic early life

The *Freeman's Journal* of 7 October 1861 announced the death from scarlatina two days previous of Joseph, a 4-year-old child of Mr Nathaniel Colgan. Mr Colgan, a pawnbroker, was then resident in Dublin's Coombe district, at 62 Cork Street. The following day the newspaper announced the death from the same ailment of Joseph's sister, Elizabeth Colgan, aged 6. True to custom, the wife and mother involved is not mentioned in either death notice. The children were 'dearly beloved'.[1] At this time the Colgan family had eight children, all living, the last born in this year of tragedy. That all survived is indictive of the comparatively comfortable state of the family. The children's father, Nathaniel *Watson* Colgan – to distinguish him from his remarkable son, the plain Nathaniel Colgan – had married Letitia Phair – sometimes written Phayer – on 24 February 1846 in St Andrew's Church (of Ireland), St Andrew's Street, Dublin.[2] This church burnt down in 1860 – along with some parish registers. It was replaced by the current structure, which has, until recently, been a tourist office. It has since become a pub. When he married Miss Phair, Nathaniel Watson Colgan was a pawnbroker's assistant, at 205 Great Britain Street, now named Parnell Street.

Letitia Phair was the daughter of John Phair, another pawnbroker, of 48 Fleet Street on the corner with Parliament Row. Griffith's Valuation of the nation's property about 1850 affirms that the Phairs were mainly in counties Fermanagh, Cavan and Cork; only three are mentioned in Dublin at that time. In contrast, fifteen Colgan tenancies were listed in Griffith's Valuation for Dublin. It appears that the bride and groom lived 'above the shop' on marriage, whereas by 1848 to 1850,[3] the couple lived at 18 Mountpleasant Avenue Lower, in Rathmines. At this time Nathaniel Watson's father, Joseph Colgan, lived at 17 Brabazon Row,[4] which abuts Weaver Street, and is near the Coombe and at the heart of the Dublin silk weavers' trade. Like many Dubliners then, they moved houses regularly. For the period 1859 to 1862 the Watson Colgans were residing at 62 Cork Street, in the

Coombe. It has since been demolished, but was probably similar to no. 72, which is extant.

When the two young children of Letitia Phair and Nathaniel Watson Colgan died – which I mentioned at the outset – the couple were aged 34 and 42 respectively, Letitia having married at the age of 19. Their surviving children were Sarah and William Henry, then aged from 1 to 2 years; Letitia, aged 8; Nathaniel, 10½; John Joseph (known to be deaf as an adult), 12; and Nannie, the eldest, 14. Within a few months of the two children's deaths from scarlet fever, their father donated £1 to Cork Street Fever Hospital. About the middle of 1862, another boy, Joseph II, was born. Eight months later, the father, Nathaniel Watson, died at his home in Bishop Street – on 23 January 1863.[5] He had been operating a pawnshop at 48 Fleet Street in the city, at the corner with Parliament Row.[6] We can presume it came with marriage to his predecessor's daughter, Letitia Phair, as her father, John Phair, had a pawnshop at this address. In July 1861 Nathaniel Watson had stretched himself financially and bought from widow Caroline Booth the existing residential pawnbrokers at 50 and 51 Bishop Street – *not surviving* – for £4,750 sterling subject to her retaining control over the buildings.[7] This suggests an income of from £290 to £475 per annum. Up to his death Nathaniel Watson Colgan had continued to operate the pawnshop at 51 Bishop Street. His widow, Letitia Colgan née Phair, took out administration of his estate. She declared that he had left an estate worth a substantial sum – but less than £7,000 – in a grant issued on 6 June 1863.[8] The following month Letitia assigned the Bishop Street property back to widow Caroline Booth with a money settlement of £401 and Letitia's right to walk away from it.

The cause of Nathaniel Watson Colgan's death at age 44 is not recorded; perhaps he had anticipated it when it was arranged that 'Messrs Bentley sell by auction today ... soft goods from the office of Mr *Nathaniel* Colgan, 51 Bishop Street ... great variety of frock, dress and walking coats, vests and trousers, silk, satin and cashmere dresses, sheets, carpets' etc.[9] This was nine months before he died. Tuberculosis suggests itself, especially given his occupation – continuously handling and storing used clothing and other belongings of the poorer classes in the city. Below is a précis of the children born to Nathaniel Watson and Letitia Phair:

Annie, aka Nannie	b. 1847; d. 23 Jan. 1916 aged 68
John Joseph	b. 1849 (deaf as an adult); d. 27 Jan. 1920 aged 70
Nathaniel	b. 28 May 1851; d. *c.*4 Oct. 1919 aged 68
Letitia	b. 1853; d. 18 Apr. 1922 aged *c.*68 at Fleetwood, Lancashire
Elizabeth	b. *c.*1855; d. 6 Oct. 1861 aged 6
Joseph (1)	b. *c.*1857; d. 5 Oct. 1861 aged 4
William Henry	b. 1860; d. 15 June 1942 aged 82
Sarah	b. 1860 or 1861; d. 31 May 1898 aged 37
Joseph (2)	b. 1862; d. 1 Mar. 1864 aged 1½

It is notable that there is neither civil nor church record existing of the birth (or baptism) of any of these children. Civil registration during this time was possible for Protestant persons where the information was volunteered. It did not become compulsory for all births to be registered until later.[10] St Luke's was the Church of Ireland parish church serving the Coombe area since 1708. It closed in 1975 and was burnt by an arsonist in 1985; some parish registers are presumed to have burned there or in the Public Record Office during the Civil War.

Of the six children of Nathaniel the elder surviving to adulthood, only one married (Revd William Henry). He had four children with his wife Constance Allman: two daughters (who married) and two sons. William's elder son, John, was born on 24 November 1889 in Seapoint House, Salthill, Galway. William, a Church of Ireland priest, was ministering, at that time, in Spiddal, a Gaeltacht area.[11] The younger son, George, was born on 4 August 1893; on 21 April 1919 he was reported killed in action in France during the First World War while serving in the 14th Australian Light Mortar Battery. Evidently George had emigrated to Australia. No evidence that George married has been located. For more on the eldest son, John, see below.

Before proceeding, it is appropriate to look at Nathaniel Watson Colgan's own generation (fig. 2). He had at least eight siblings, most of whom died young and unmarried. His father was Joseph Colgan, a silk weaver and, sometimes, a silk manufacturer. Joseph was born in 1792 and he died 27 November 1878 aged 86 years.[12] He was Church of Ireland by religion, and his family lived at New Row South, in the Coombe area. Later he moved to 17 Brabazon Row, also in the

Nathaniel Colgan *fl.*1791

Joseph Colgan = Elizabeth Watson (?)
1792–1878

Nathaniel Watson = Letitia Phair
1818–63   (d. 1865)
m. 1846

Maryanne
b. 1820

Joseph = Sarah Andrews
1822–64   m. Robert A Rowan
m. 1854   1875

Elizabeth
b. 1824

William
b. 1827

Margaret = Patk Downes
b. 1829
m. 1854

Sarah
b. 1831–1909

William
1834–5

Henry
1838–58

Annie
1847–1916

John Joseph
1849–1920

Nathaniel
1851–1919

Letitia
1853–1922

Elizabeth
1855–61

Joseph I
1857–61

Wm Henry = Constance Allman
1860–1942   1858–1945
m. 1888

Sarah
1860/61–98

Joseph II
1862–4

John (Jack) = Eliz Harriet
1889–1959   Worthington
m (1) 1916

Constance Mary = George Cameron
1892–1958

George
1893–1918
KIA

Godfrey Clarke = Hilda Anne
1897–1956
m. 1920

Elizabeth L
b. 1922

m (2) 1944   Mollie Ralton

2. Family tree for five generations of Nathaniel Colgan's family

3. Family gravestone in Mount Jerome Cemetery, Dublin

Coombe. There is a record of another Nathaniel Colgan flourishing in Dublin in 1791; Joseph may be his son, as Joseph's eldest son was called Nathaniel Watson Colgan. The numerous records have obdurately not revealed the children's mother Elizabeth's maiden name but it is likely she was a Watson as her eldest son bore that as a middle name. Moreover, Colgans and Watsons were neighbours in the Coombe district (and in Co. Offaly).

Joseph outlived all but one – Sarah – of his nine children. He died of chronic bronchitis in the Old Men's Asylum, Rathmines,[13] and he is commemorated on his grandson Nathaniel Colgan the naturalist's family gravestone, no. 13082, in Mount Jerome Cemetery, Dublin (fig. 3). This gravestone is the only comprehensive record to hand of the family line. Nathaniel was a careful annotator, usually in his minuscule handwriting.

We can speculate how Joseph Colgan became a silk weaver and why he was a Protestant. Weaving as a craft was commonly practised in fifteenth-century Ireland, and other family lore has it that skilled weavers moved from rural Westmeath into Dublin; that is likely to be true of other counties contiguous to the capital. Joseph Colgan, or probably his forebears, had migrated to Dublin to become silk weavers, most likely from Offaly, Kildare or Westmeath, where the Colgan surname was most prominent in 1901. In the late 1600s French Huguenots, who were Protestants fleeing persecution under the French Catholic king, became established in Dublin. Many settled in the Liberties. They were experienced silk weavers and had a great dislike of the Catholic Church. A weavers' hall was built in the Lower Coombe in 1682, and when a new one was required in 1745, the money was advanced by a Huguenot banker, David Digges La

Touche. It was 56 feet long by 21 feet wide. Huguenot names soon disappeared from among the names of weavers. In 1771, there were 1,200 silk looms and a Weavers' Guild that regulated training and entry to the business. They were also represented on the city council. The guild had the effect of creating a 'closed shop', restricted to, inter alia, Protestants. The protection provided by the guild waned, however, as many Catholics operated illegally and without sanction. Some artefacts belonging to the guild have survived, including an oak chest, now in the Metropolitan Museum of New York. It has these words inscribed on it: 'This is the Corporation of Weavers' Chest ann. 1706 – *Nathaniel* James, Master; William Pierce and Thomas Howe, Wardens'. The weavers' hall was demolished in 1965.[14] The rebellion of 1798 ruined many of the silk weavers and the business went into decline, with some weavers moving to Lisburn and Belfast.

Joseph Colgan probably set up his children as pawnbrokers. He and his wife Elizabeth's children, in order of their birth dates, were:

Nathaniel Watson	b. 4 Dec. 1818; d. 23 Jan. 1863
Maryanne	b. 5 Aug. 1820; 'Widow Sullivan' in 1901 at 63.7 Dominick St.
Joseph	b. 3 Oct. 1822; d. in 1864, after 10 years married to Sarah Andrews
Elizabeth	b. 14 Sept. 1824
William I	b. 12 Jan. 1827; d. young
Margaret	b. 23 Apr. 1829; married Patrick Downes, 19 Sept. 1854 in Catholic church
Sarah	b. 27 Oct. 1831; d. 9 Jan. 1909, s.p., 8 Charlemont Mall with nephew (?) Sullivan
William II	b. 26 Apr. 1834; d. 30 Aug. 1835
Henry	b. 21 Sept. 1838; d. 21 Apr. 1858 aged 19, at Brabazon Row

Of significance from a deep-genealogy perspective is continuity in the male line so that DNA testing of living male descendants can reveal their ancient and predominantly rural origins.[15] Of the nine siblings mentioned, Nathaniel Watson and Joseph were the only males who survived into marriage. Joseph died after ten years of marriage,

4. Nathaniel Colgan's birth-home: 8 Bell's Vista, Heytesbury Street, Dublin

leaving no record of any children to him and his wife, Sarah Andrews. She remarried a widower, Robert Alex Rowan.

More tragedy was to befall the Colgan family of Nathaniel Watson and Letitia. Now without a breadwinner, they moved into Rehoboth House, Dolphin's Barn. This was a Protestant reformatory school – and they were Protestants – together with Rehoboth Cottage, which served as a sheltered home for impecunious Protestants.[16] Rehoboth House was near Cork Street. Their infant child, Joseph II, died there on 1 March 1864 aged about 1½ years. The following spring the morning newspaper of 28 April 1865 carried this death notice:

> DEATH April 23, at her residence, Rehoboth House, SCR, after a long and painful illness, to the inexpressible grief of her young family, Letitia, relict of Mr Nathaniel *Watson* Colgan, and daughter of the late Mr John Phair. Her remains will be removed for interment at 9 o'clock on tomorrow Saturday morning. Friends will please accept this intimation.[17]

She, Nathaniel's mother, was interred in her family plot, no. 476, in Mount Jerome Cemetery.

Nathaniel Watson Colgan and family were a relatively prosperous pawnbroking family in the 1840s, as is evident from Nathaniel the younger's birth-home: 8 Bell's Vista, Heytesbury Street, in St Peter's parish, Dublin (fig. 4).[18] This is an end-of-terrace house facing the Meath Hospital. The children were now reduced to orphans dependant on Protestant protection, their aged grandfather (73), and whoever else in the family would take care of them. They did have, however, a substantial inheritance. Nathaniel Colgan, the subject of this monograph, was by then almost 14 years of age.

TRACING NATHANIEL COLGAN'S ROOTS

Interested in my own genealogy after being given my own Dublin Colgan family's seminal papers going back to about 1814, I attended a genealogy congress or fair in London about twenty years ago. I was persuaded to do a 37-marker male-DNA test at the stand of FamilyTreeDNA.com by the president of the company, who was behind the desk. FTdna was the first company in the world to do DNA testing of males as an aid to tracing a family's line, and they were then the biggest company in this field. Shortly afterwards I agreed to become the voluntary administrator of a Colgan surname project with the company and since then I have gathered specific DNA data on over thirty Colgan male participants in Ireland, Britain and America, linking some to each other, and some to areas within Ireland. As the name is Gaelic and occupational (meaning, in short: 'swordsman', from *colg*), separate clans of that name could be established anywhere. Knowing that the 'Colgan intensity', i.e., the number of Colgans in the population per 100,000, in the available censuses was largest in Co. Offaly (formerly known as King's County), I set to find Colgan males in the county who would do the DNA test. Using the DNA tool, I first found a close DNA match with a male Colgan from the townland of Clonbrin, Clonsast civil parish, Co. Offaly. From him and his cousin, I learned of the family's recent history in the area. Subsequently I located the marriage record of my Colgan ancestor who migrated to Dublin about 1812; he was married in Clonbulloge

Roman Catholic parish church. Clonbulloge townland is a subset of Clonsast civil parish. Clonbulloge (and Clonsast) are very close to the town of Rathangan, Co. Kildare. The contemporary translation of Clonbulloge is via the Gaelic words, *Cluain* – meaning meadow – and *Bolg*, meaning swollen, or bulging (as an adjective); in English this is usually interpreted as 'bumpy meadow'. After visiting the location, I found Clonbulloge as a flat plain – fit for an airfield – and thus this combination becomes irreconcilable with that. Referring to Dinneen's *Irish-English dictionary* (1927 edition), I found this on p. 140:

> *Bhullaidh*, an Ulster word for the foreigner or Williamite (from Willie), often written Wooly; so the combination becomes: *clann Bhullaidh*, the foreign settlers in Ulster [*Wooly is also how an Ulster person might pronounce Willie*].

After consulting Seamus Cullen MA PhD, a local historian of several decades' acquaintance who is very knowledgeable of this area, and telling him of my hypothesis – of which he was unaware – that this area had been settled by Williamite planters, he said he had researched the Watson family for his MA dissertation, interviewing them. They descended from a Colonel Tom Watson who took part in King William's campaign in Ireland in the 1690s, and purchased land from the local owners before settling there. They came from Cumberland. Watson became a Quaker. The local Quakers had meeting houses in Rathangan and Edenderry and a cemetery in Rathangan where many Watsons are interred. After a baby was born out of wedlock, the Quaker elders put one of the Watsons out of their community. The Watsons then gave up being Quakers. Two of them moved to Dublin and, according to Dr Cullen, set up a business, 'The Spinning Wheel', at 30 New Row, Thomas Street. This is an error; New Row South is off the Coombe. They re-joined the Quakers in 1793. Cullen's story of the Watsons of Baltracey was published in 1999 in *Oughterany*, an occasional local history journal in north-west Kildare. It is also on that author's website.[19] With the passing of the land acts, the Colgans of Clonbrin townland in Clonsast civil parish purchased most of the land in the area, including the 'big house' where one of them resided. In Griffith's General Valuation (*c.*1850), eleven of the twenty-three

Watson owner-occupiers of properties in King's County were in Clonsast civil parish.

I sought to find a male Colgan descendant of Joseph Colgan (1792–1878), or either of the two Nathaniels, father and son, and so on. Unfortunately, only one male that I could trace remained from these families: Dr John, Nathaniel's nephew. John Colgan had passed his final medical exams in TCD in the spring of 1912 – the only candidate who passed 'on high marks'. He passed his surgery component in June that year.[20] He obtained work in Fleetwood, Lancashire, on or near qualification, but he returned to Dublin to marry Elizabeth Harriet Worthington in St James' Church of Ireland church, Dublin, on 25 January 1916. His bride was from *Winton*, SCR, Kilmainham; the marriage was solemnized by the groom's father, Revd William Henry Colgan. The marriage was not registered in the Irish General Register's Office (GRO) at the time, as required by law. I have found no children of the marriage registered in the Irish GRO. On their marriage, the couple returned to the seaside town of Fleetwood, Lancashire, to Dr Colgan's job. English newspapers report on the doctor's annual reports of the health of his district and so on. The English GRO records one birth to the new Mrs Colgan, of a daughter, Elizabeth L., born in the second quarter of 1922, in the Fylde district of Lancashire. Fylde includes Fleetwood and Lytham St Anne's.[21] There is no other record of a Colgan birth in that district up to 1936. Dr John Colgan died aged 69 on 19 June 1959, without a male heir, as far as I can ascertain.[22] For the time being, a DNA trace on these Colgans, or Watson Colgans is in abeyance.

There is an established pattern of historic migration from the counties close to the west and north-west side of Dublin into the Thomas Street–James Street area to work and to establish businesses there. On the basis of circumstantial evidence – and until one has DNA facts – I will hold that Nathaniel Colgan's Watson links are from Clonsast civil parish, and his Colgan links likewise.

2. Schooling and the day job

At this time, and even later, priority was given to the schooling of Protestant boys. At the time of their mother's death (1865), there were three boys surviving: John Joseph (16), Nathaniel (14) and William Henry (5). John Joseph was classified as deaf in the census of 1901 by his brother, Nathaniel, who was also deemed 'head of household', and John was not gainfully employed; there is no evidence to hand of his schooling. The Protestant community provided scholarships for Protestant boys to receive a particular kind of schooling 'under the patronage of the Incorporated Society for the Promotion of English Protestant Schools in Ireland' – they were known as charter schools. Girls were not treated equally. While Nathaniel and his brother, William – later to be Revd William – lived on the campus of Rehoboth reformatory school, we know nothing of their very early schooling. However, the newspapers are peppered with teachers called Colgan – married, unmarried, both genders – and Colgan pupils who made it into print in their exam results. Nathaniel appears in meritorious terms in the annual results for the Dublin English, Scientific and Commercial Day School, at 55 Aungier Street – beside Whitefriars' Street Carmelite convent and church, and now a cafeteria (fig. 5). At the Christmas examinations held over three days in 1863, Nathaniel – now 12½ and in Class 4 – won first prize in English, according to John Holmes, the headmaster and a TCD Scholar.[1] By the summer of 1869, Nathaniel (18), by now at Mr Johnston's Academy on Gardiner Place, sat the recent examinations of the Royal Dublin Society. They awarded him a certificate of merit for general subjects, geography and English history. He was also awarded the second prize of £1 for English history and geography.[2]

In August 1870, the UK government decided that all junior positions in the civil service were to be filled by open competition. It held the first competition on 28 February 1871 to fill twenty positions. Seventy-four candidates contested, of whom twenty-five were Irish. English candidates won twelve positions (corresponding to

5. Dublin English, Scientific and Commercial Day School, 55 Aungier Street, Dublin, October 2019

a 24 per cent success rate) and Irish ones the remaining eight places (32 per cent success rate). Of these eight, four were from Mr Johnston's Academy, Gardiner Place: Nathaniel Colgan, Rehoboth House, SCR, plus another Dubliner, and two young men from Tralee.[3] In another competition that year for cadetship in the constabulary, there were nine successful candidates in all Ireland. Johnston announced that four were his; among them Nathaniel Colgan of Dublin, who took seventh place of seventy-four candidates.[4] Looking as though he was not fully satisfied with what he had been offered to date, Nathaniel Colgan made another attempt in 1871, sitting the open competition examinations on 25 October 1871 for twenty civil service clerkships. Government official papers report that he secured 1,958 total marks (75.3 per cent) out of a possible 2,600, coming in fifth place.[5] The *Londonderry Standard* reported on the outcome of the open competition for Higher Offices. The Dubliner, Downer, came first in the British Isles and was appointed to the Board of Trade,

London; Nathaniel Colgan came second of the Irish candidates and
was appointed to the Metropolitan Justices' Courts, Dublin, a post
of his own choosing.[6] He had been prepared for the Metropolitan
Justices' Court in Mr Johnston's Gardiner Place Academy.[7] He was
now aged 20. That ended his formal, full-time education and training.
Thereafter, he was self-taught in botany and additional languages,
other than those which he may have been coached in by his younger
brother, William, a brilliant linguist at Dublin University, and on-
the-job training at his single, working career in the courts.

Obviously Nathaniel Colgan must have had some interest in the
legal profession, which gave him reason to choose a civil service job
as a law clerk. As a child, he would have heard tales from his father
and mother of persons pawning stolen goods or goods obtained by
deception in their shops, being caught by his father or grandfather
and their participation in the ensuing court cases. The newspapers
reported on such cases.[8] He most likely chose to take a job as soon
as practicable after college to provide for his family of siblings, he
being effectively the main bread-winner among them. He continued
as court clerk at Inns' Quay for the remainder of his working life and
rose to be chief clerk in the Dublin police court (1902). There was
the occasional case in which he would be mentioned that reached
the newspapers. For example, in 1912 a controversial case took
place, which was to be transferred to a superior court. It involved
sending the record of the proceedings for a review and *habeas corpus*
on behalf of four suffragettes who were detained in Mountjoy prison
after conviction by Mr Swifte, the chief divisional magistrate, for
having broken windows in the city of Dublin. The suffragettes were
Margaret Palmer, Jane Murphy, Hannah Sheehy-Skeffington and
Margaret Murphy. Affidavits were put in by officials of the police
court, the first of which was from Nathaniel Colgan, the chief clerk.[9]

Contemporary commentators said he never sought to advance
himself in the job beyond that and instead developed parallel
interests, in some of which he excelled. He was an autodidact;
this may have been facilitated by his being shy, it is said, and by his
remaining unmarried all his life. I believe he kept quiet about his
early life and background in the company of peers more privileged
than he in scientific circles. All his surviving siblings – with whom he
lived – remained single. His younger brother, William Henry, was an

exception. William married a professor's daughter after his university education in Trinity College Dublin, where he excelled as a linguist – including a Gaelic one – and became a Church of Ireland minister. On the occasion of his golden wedding anniversary, aged 78 or 79, William was said to have spoken seven languages fluently.[10]

During his early years as a court clerk, Nathaniel took part in the Civil Service Sports' Club annual games at Leinster Cricket Ground, being placed in the 150 yards hurdle race over 10 hurdles in two successive years.[11] Thereafter we hear no more of that, as he turned to mountaineering here and abroad and to the quiet, painstaking work of recording the flora in the county of Dublin. He is said to have walked over every mountain range in Ireland, often with Dubliner Charles Frederick D'Arcy, with his brother William, both clerics and classmates at Trinity College Dublin, and with a much younger man, Kinsley D. Doyle, an engineer. They were all enthralled by the wild. As well as Ireland they mountaineered in Scotland, Wales, the Alps and elsewhere. D'Arcy was later to become a bishop of the Church of Ireland at Clogher (1903–7), of Ossory, Ferns and Leighlin followed by Down, Connor and Dromore, briefly of Dublin and finally of Armagh from 1920 until his death.[12] D'Arcy's maternal grandfather was Thomas Brierly, the owner or occupier of Rehoboth House. Nathaniel met D'Arcy, another botanist, as he too lodged at Rehoboth House. The two men also climbed on the European continent.[13] William was often with them on the mountains, sometimes looking for plants. Nathaniel was also a photographer of some note, winning prizes for his scenery pictures and occasionally he put on lantern slide shows for the public.[14]

Later, as chief court clerk, Nathaniel is seen to deal with mundane matters: to send condolences and to attend funerals of magistrates, constabulary and officials connected with his job. He also got to visit the residential industrial school for boys run by the Oblate Community in Glencree, Co. Wicklow, once a year, accompanied by the lord mayor and other dignitaries, after which they were treated. I have no reports of his observations, if any. Judging by his acquaintances' observations of him as a quiet or shy man, exemplified by how long it took him to make his first presentation in the RIA, by the nature of his job, and by his not being a Roman Catholic, I would expect him to be discrete.[15]

3. Interest in Irish language and culture

In an anonymous obituary on Nathaniel Colgan's death, the *Irish Times* writer claimed that 'He had a wonderful facility for languages, German, French, Danish, Norwegian and Swedish, and he was a first-rate Irish scholar. He corresponded even with Japanese naturalists'.[1]

At a public meeting held in the Mansion House, Dublin, on 4 April 1895 with the lord mayor presiding, it was resolved to hold a Festival of Irish Music in Dublin as soon as practicable, lasting four days, and to be known by the Gaelic word, *Feis*. It was to include a concert of ancient Irish music, an orchestral concert of music by modern Irish composers, choir and band contests, the performance of prize compositions and lectures on Irish music. The organizers hoped that it would be held periodically in Irish cities. A fund was set up to which Dr Walsh, the Roman Catholic archbishop of Dublin, donated £10 10s.; Lord Plunket, the Church of Ireland archbishop, donated £10; Nathaniel Colgan, MRIA, £5 – the next largest donation – and G.F. FitzGerald FTCD, £2 2s. etc. The committee for the proposed *feis* had written a letter to the newspaper soliciting financial support, or guarantees of support should the revenue be insufficient. A list of those (27) who subscribed and those who went guarantor was subsequently published in the *Freeman's Journal* on 13 March 1896; among the latter was Nathaniel Colgan MRIA for £5.[2]

It was another year before the *Feis Ceoil* was held. Its success was noted at a lecture on 'The Irish contribution to the British drama', held in the Leinster Lecture Hall, Molesworth Street, Dublin, under the auspices of the National Literary Society. Nathaniel Colgan and 'Miss Colgan' attended, but is not clear which of his three sisters accompanied him. Dr Sigerson, who presided at the lecture, remarked on the great success some members of the society and others had in establishing a *Feis Ceoil* during the past week. A list of many persons of Irish origin or residence who contributed to the *Feis Ceoil* was provided in the newspaper.[3] Nathaniel was among those present at the October 1897 general meeting in connection with the *Feis Ceoil*, which took place in the Oak Room of the Mansion House, Dublin. The meeting was held to make arrangements for the next festival and for electing honorary officers and nominating the central executive.[4] The city mayor was obviously aware of Nathaniel's part: in May 1899 the mayor gave a *conversazione* in the Mansion House in honour of members of the *Feis Ceoil* and invited a distinguished company to meet them. Mr Colgan and Miss Colgan were among the invitees.[5]

Nathaniel also contributed to the language movement – to the Irish Language National Fund, operated by the Gaelic League, of which he had been elected a member.[6] His brother, William, belonged to the Irish Society, which promulgated the Bible *as Gaeilge*.[7]

Nathaniel was not shy of singing in public – certainly later in life. He and two others – Messrs Lawlor and Clarke – are on record as providing a vocal trio at a concert in the Coffee Palace, Townsend Street, Dublin, at which 'an Edison's phonograph session and 200 slides, lit by a powerful oxy-hydrogen apparatus', were shown.[8] He was involved in putting on several slide shows, usually based on his preoccupation with plant and sea life, and he was a member of the Kingstown Photographic Society and exhibited with the society. I have not located records of that society.

NATURAL HISTORY

The Dublin Naturalists' Field Club was founded in the summer of 1886. No qualifications were required for membership. It had a general aim of promoting all branches of natural history, and a particular aim in the conservation and protection of scarce and threatened plants and animals, along with the protection of sites of scientific interest. Its first president was Prof. Perceval Wright, who was later to be a proposer of Nathaniel's membership of the Royal Irish Academy. Nathaniel joined it this year. Robert Lloyd Praeger, the Co. Down engineer by profession, librarian by occupation and naturalist by inclination, also joined it in the inaugural year. Colgan and he became friends and colleagues. Later in life, Praeger founded An Taisce, the National Trust.

The bachelor Colgan, with the long vacation periods only enjoyed by the legal profession, universities, courts and parliament, was able to devote a lot of his life to his inclination towards natural history. He played leading roles in the Dublin Naturalists' Field Club, the Irish Naturalists' Field Club and the Irish Cosmos Club. In 1896, Nathaniel was appointed vice-president of the Dublin Naturalists' Field Club, and Praeger honorary secretary. In this year, in this capacity, he put on an exhibition for St Patrick's Day in the botanical branch of the Science and Art Museum of flowering and other growing shamrocks. After moving to 15 Breffni Terrace (*c*.1900), a substantial end-of-terrace, three-storey house in Glasthule, and facing Bullock Harbour, he began taking an interest in marine biology. The Field Club took a trip to Lambay off Rush, Co. Dublin, in 1905 and with the encouragement of the owner carried out surveys of all the natural life there. This was followed by a series of lectures in 1907, invariably at the premises of the Royal Irish Academy on Dawson Street. Colgan, who had uncovered seventy-seven species of mollusc as his contribution to the expedition, gave a lecture on them. At the AGM of the Dublin Naturalists' Field Club in June 1914, he was elected president of the club; his presidency was renewed in 1915. His talks were not without humour, exemplified by his singing at his lantern shows. Following his trips to the Pyrenees in July 1880 and July 1883, he gave an illustrated talk entitled 'Plant hunting in the Pyrenees' (February 1912).

He was elected a Member of the Royal Irish Academy in 1894, when he was neither a university graduate nor an academic by occupation. His membership was proposed by George Noble Plunkett and seconded by six others – Alexander Goodman More, Greenwood Pim, Richard Manliffe Barrington, Revd Thomas Olden, Revd Samuel Hemphill and Prof. Edward Perceval Wright. His candidature was certified on 12 March 1894 and his election was confirmed on 9 April.[9]

G.N. Plunkett (1851–1948), Colgan's contemporary, was born in Dublin of a Norman-Irish family; he was a biographer and a papal count, and he was educated both in Ireland and abroad; he became a nationalist and Sinn Féin supporter; later an independent MP. Goodman More (1830–95) was born in London and probably lived in Rathmines where his sister (and, for a time, Nathaniel) lived;

a Cambridge drop-out and a naturalist, his job was as curator of the Natural History Museum, Dublin; and with David Moore, director of the Botanic Gardens, Glasnevin, he was an author of *Cybele Hibernica* (1866). Goodman More's sister, Frances, lived on Leinster Road, Rathmines. On More's demise, she funded a project undertaken by Colgan and Reginald Scully of Kerry to update the *Cybele* out of moneys left by her brother in his will. It was More who urged Nathaniel Colgan to pursue his most enduring and most famous work, *Flora of the county Dublin*. We rarely hear of Nathaniel's sisters participating in his life, but exceptionally we note that his youngest sister, Sarah, ten years his junior and who died aged 37 of tuberculosis, did extensive field work with him in the Fingal area. His sister, Letitia, two years his junior, and who outlived all the Colgan siblings, also did field work in Howth, in Vesey's Lucan Demesne, and near his residence in Sandycove. So too did his younger brother, the Revd William.

Greenwood Pim MA (TCD) (d. 14 November 1906) was a Quaker resident of Monkstown, Co. Dublin, and was secretary of the conjoint board of the Royal Colleges of Surgeons and Physicians. R.M. Barrington MA (TCD) (1849–1915) was born near Bray, Co. Wicklow; he was a naturalist, a farmer and a valuer. He wrote on the flora of the Blasket Islands, Co. Kerry, and went on the RIA's Rockall expedition with Praeger. Thomas Olden (1823–1900) was a Church of Ireland priest, a biographer and contributor to the *Dictionary of national biography* (UK). Samuel Hemphill, a Presbyterian minister, was descended from the Hemphills of Co. Tipperary, where he resided.

Perceval Wright (1834–1910) was a surgeon, a botanist and a zoologist. He was taught natural history by George Allman, Revd William Colgan's father-in-law. Wright was the curator of TCD's museum and professor of botany there for decades.

Colgan translated his love of the Irish language into his hobbies: plant and sea-animal life. In 1911 he submitted a short report, 'Irish names of animals and plants', to the Royal Irish Academy meeting due to be held on 27 February[10] and in the same year he published 'Clare Island Survey: Gaelic plant and animal names'.[11] He gave a second paper on Irish names of animals and plants, which he gathered from the country folk and fishermen of Clare Island and the mainland shores of Clew Bay. The precise species were also determined and numerous variants of the names were added, based on the author's researches elsewhere in Ireland.[12] Despite being sixteen years a member of the RIA, this was his first paper to the academy. Shyness is the explanation offered. However, when his unknown family background is considered, it is possible that it was an inferiority complex in the company of high-flying academics, or perceived professional snobbery associated with them, that bothered him more.

After Colgan's election to the RIA, Academy House became the regular venue for meetings of the Dublin Naturalists' Field Club, of which he was a founder member. The *Irish Naturalist* of March 1914 carried a reproduction in full of Colgan's presidential address to the Dublin Naturalists' Field Club on the folklore of Irish plants and animals.[13] Irish names for the various plants and animals were printed in Celtic characters (that is, the *cló Gaelach* characters commonly used in Irish writing of the day and until around 1952, when Irish text switched to the *cló Rómhánach*). A newspaper reviewer asserted that the article was one of the most readable that the journal has produced.[14] In a similar manner, he examined the influence of the Vikings on plant names. On the publication of his magnum opus, *Flora of the county Dublin*, in 1904, Nathaniel wrote that he had not discovered any trace of Scandinavian plant names in Dublin, which 'reinforces the already strong negative evidence that the Danes nowhere became fused with the Irish'.[15] He, and they, are in error here: the Vikings who settled here were mainly of Norwegian, rather than of Danish origin. Besides, there was no distinction in their era between the modern states of Scandinavia. Most recent DNA studies suggest that being a Viking was more of an occupational status than a nationality. Moreover, contrary to Nathaniel's assertion, they did integrate with the Gaelic Irish, as is evident from the many hybrid Viking-Gaelic names, such as McAuley, which prevailed in public office in Dublin and elsewhere shortly after the Anglo-Norman encroachment on Ireland.[16]

The Gaelic League was established in 1893 as a successor to several bodies with overlapping aims. It was 'founded solely to keep the Irish language spoken in Ireland'. Later, many of its followers were to become overtly nationalistic. This led to the imperial establishment being suspicious of those who became members. Its first president

(1893–1915) was a Protestant, Dr Douglas Hyde, which lent credence to the notion that it was a cultural rather than a political organization. Somewhat surprisingly, Nathaniel Colgan, at the age of 47, applied to join the league, then at 4 College Green, Dublin. At a meeting of the Executive Committee of the league held on 21 February 1899, Colgan's application was accepted, and the matter was reported in the *Freeman's Journal* newspaper. A public meeting was held on the following day. There was a large attendance, and it was chaired by its president, Douglas Hyde.[17]

NATHANIEL COLGAN AND THE SHAMROCK

Among the most enduring endeavours of Nathaniel Colgan were his surveys in 1892 and 1893 to see what plant was worn on St Patrick's Day – an immovable feast in the Christian calendar, 17 March each year.[18] St Patrick is regarded by people around the globe as the patron saint of Ireland. Surprisingly, he is not recognized as being in the same saintly league as his female peer, St Brigid, by the Church of Rome.

After St Patrick's Day 1892, Nathaniel Colgan (40), the Dublin police court clerk in his 'day job', sent out a circular letter (three dozen) to recipients in Irish-speaking districts, mostly to parish priests in various counties of Ireland, asking them to send him a sample of the typical plant worn on St Patrick's Day that year – by men on the hat, not the lapel – complete with root-ball and soil. Eight responded with specimens – just over 20 per cent. By modern standards, a 20 per cent return on a mail-shot survey would be considered good. The following year he adopted a different approach and gathered many more specimens. Seven counties (including Kildare) remained outside his enquiry. Each specimen was examined and grown into flower to confirm the accuracy of its botanical name. Out of a total of 49 duly authenticated, 24 proved to be *trifolium repens*, white clover, 21 to be *trifolium minus*, now known as *trifolium dubium*, yellow or dwarf clover, 2 to be *trifolium pratense*, red clover, and 2 to be *medicago lupulina*, black clover. Colgan added to previous enquiries made by British botanist James Britten, editor of the *Journal of Botany*, to strengthen the claim that *trifolium minus* was the favoured plant as the national symbol in most districts, as it remains to the present day. All the plant varieties belong to the bean family – *Leguminosae*, now known as *Fabaceae*. All 'fix' the otherwise inert nitrogen gas they take from the air and combine it internally with hydrogen and oxygen to make ammonia, nitrates and nitrites. These chemicals serve to make the ground more fertile. However, some of them leach into water courses to cause eutrophication.[19]

Colgan suggested – probably with tongue in cheek – that a jury of experts ought to rule on which would be the 'true shamrock'. In the end the market decided in favour of the dwarf or yellow clover. Colgan's choice of the yellow clover was backed up by the findings of Britten, who wrote in 1920 that

> Many years ago, when he and the late Robert Holland were compiling their Dictionary of English Plant-names, they went into the matter with some care, obtaining specimens from many Irish counties and examining plants sold in Covent Garden and elsewhere. In the former case, the little yellow trefoil, known as *trifolium minus*, was always sent, and what were sold in the markets belonged to the same species, though the common white clover was sometimes employed as a substitute.[20]

As mentioned earlier, Nathaniel Colgan had befriended Robin [Robert] Praeger, an engineer from Co. Down who had worked for the Belfast Water Works, before he turned his mind to library duties and to botany. Praeger, Prof. George H. Carpenter and other naturalists in April 1892 started the *Irish Naturalist* magazine, which the pair edited. Nathaniel published his preliminary 'real shamrock' research in it in August 1892. The quirky nature of his article led to many newspapers and other publications reproducing it.[21] The fact that a Protestant Colgan family of prize-winning gunsmiths and cutlers from Limerick, reputed to be of Offaly stock, and who had married into a family in the shipping business at Hull, may be the reason for the faraway *Hull Daily Mail*'s strange interest in Irish affairs and the shamrock. The *Daily Telegraph* printed an amusing tongue-in-cheek report on it:

> Politicians have inflicted many grievances upon Ireland, but the latest and greatest of all comes from the hands of the men of

science. They have proved that a great mass of Irishmen living in their own country do not really know what the true shamrock is. Mr Nathaniel Colgan and Mr R.L. Praeger have been investigating the subject on the spot, and obtained from native experts the plants recognized by the inhabitants of 13 counties as the one and only true shamrock.

'Armagh and Carlow were evenly divided against themselves' preferring one, or another, variety of shamrock. 'A country divided against itself on the national emblem cannot be expected to be harmonious respecting a form of government' it declared.[22] The *Irish Naturalist*'s article led the *London Daily News* to comment: 'It will strike the Saxon reader as odd that there should still be any doubt as to the exact identity of this cherished national emblem'.[23]

Nathaniel set about researching early mentions of the shamrock and when it was first connected with the patron saint of the isle. His trawl of the published literature must have been onerous without either computer or world-wide-web. Nevertheless, the Victorians and earlier generations were excellent at keeping records. He found that the shamrock's history was essentially in two phases: first, when it was used as a herb or a food up to 1680, when Henry Mundy wrote on the topic.[24] Thereafter a cross-over period ensued when it was used both as a food and as an emblem, and finally it became used as an emblem alone. Because of the scattered nature of the written records, Nathaniel Colgan found it convenient to create a chronology of seminal events. This he published in two parts in consecutive quarterly issues of the *Journal of the Royal Society of Antiquaries of Ireland*, in 1896.[25] Colgan's trawl of the literature revealed the first written record of the wearing of the shamrock on St Patrick's Day in the journal of Thomas Dineley also known as *Dingley*, gentleman, in 1687:

17th day of March yearly is St Patrick's, an immoveable feast, when the Irish of all stations and conditions wear crosses in their hats, some of pins, some of green ribbon and the vulgar superstitiously wear shamrogues, three leaved grass which they likewise eat (they say to cause a sweet breath). The common people and servants also demand their Patrick's groat of their masters which they go expressly to town, though half a dozen miles off, to spend … and very few of the zealous are found sober at night.

But the correspondent writes that earlier literature contains many interesting references to the plant. Edmund Spenser (*c.*1552–99), a London-born poet who settled in Munster after engaging in the recent war, provided one such reference of interest. In his 'A view of the present state of Ireland' (1596), he described the wealth of Munster in corn and cattle before the war; during the war, a 'scorched-earth' policy was adopted in order to supress the second Desmond Rebellion (1579–83). He wrote that the unfortunate, starving inhabitants now 'flock to a plot of water-cresses or shamrocks as to a feast'.[26]

The first printed reference to the then current tradition of claiming that St Patrick made use of the three-leafed shamrock to explain the mystery of the holy trinity is in Caleb Threlkeld's book, *Short treatise on native plants* (1727). In his next sentence, Threlkeld wrote that those celebrating generally drank to excess on the day, leading to debauchery. A surgeon, Dr William Frazer MRIA, a Fellow of the Royal Society of Antiquaries of Ireland, anticipated Nathaniel's enquiries and wrote (1894) that a learned Irish scholar informed him that *samaróg* – shamrock – means the *early* summer plant, being derived from *samradh*, summer, and *óg*, young.[27] Hence, shamrock became the familiar name for the plant, which is really a clover.

Colgan was fond of donating specimens to Irish and British museums. In 1896 the Science and Art Museum, Dublin, reported: 'The Museum is indebted to Mr N. Colgan MRIA, vice-president of the Dublin Naturalists' Field Club, for an exhibit of mounted specimens in flower of shamrock in the botanical department'.[28] They were exhibited repeatedly over the years. The Dublin daily newspapers of St Patrick's Day 1910 reported that 'Examples of shamrock are on exhibition in the botanical division of the National Museum, based on enquiry into the nature of the shamrock by Mr N. Colgan MRIA'.[29] And they were exhibited again in 1911.[30] In 1926

St Patrick's Day visitors to the National Museum will find on exhibition in the reopened Botanical Division a case containing named living specimens and the set made by the late N. Colgan of the several species of plants which work as shamrock and received by him from various counties of Ireland.[31]

Colgan's research did not extend to Ireland's or Britain's coinage. Early Irish coins, going back to Norman times, often had three raised circles – pellets – in each quadrant round a cross on them. I am advised by Edward Colgan, coin collector and author on Irish coinage, that these were not, as is sometimes claimed, images of shamrock.[32] In 1926 the Irish Free State government established a committee to advise on the design of new coinage. It was under the chair of poet William Butler Yeats. Yeats' group decided not to replicate stereotypical images of Ireland, including the shamrock. Instead, they chose Irish animals, leaving out the wolfhound, already well-worn as typifying Ireland. For a variety of reasons, some traders also made token coins that would be exchanged for 'real' money in the Bank of Ireland. One such was James Hilles, an ironmonger of 95 Abbey Street, Dublin, with a residence at the Bridge House, Leixlip. He owned the iron mills at Leixlip and leased several houses in the town, presumably for his workers. Hilles' halfpenny token shows, on the front, two men using mill-powered rollers on bar iron and 'J. Hilles – Dublin', and on the obverse, a large sprig of shamrock and the assuring message: 'Payable in Bank of Ireland Notes 1813'.

4. Magnum opus:
Flora of the county Dublin

The Londoner, Alexander Gordon More, and David Moore, the Scot who was director of the Botanic Gardens, Glasnevin, for decades, completed their oddly named book, *Cybele Hibernica*, an outline of the geographical distribution of plants in Ireland, in 1866. Cybele was the Roman goddess of wild nature. More was the curator in Dublin's Natural History Museum, and there befriended Nathaniel Colgan when the latter was aged about 30. He encouraged Colgan to compile an inventory and distribution of the wild plants in his native county, Dublin. Colgan had been bringing in samples of his plant finds on the mountains of Ireland, which he climbed with his bishop pal and others, for classification and identification. In 1892 Nathaniel began in earnest spending his weekends and spare time cycling and taking bus and train to far-flung parts of the county, sometimes with one or more of his siblings – sisters Letitia, Sarah and 'Miss'; and his brother, William – in search of plants which he also transplanted to his garden at home.[1] Occasionally, as he made new discoveries, he would publish the details in *The Irish Naturalist*.[2] More asked Nathaniel and Dr Reginald Scully – a non-practising physician from Kerry and as besotted with wild plants in Kerry as Colgan was elsewhere – to bring out a new edition of *Cybele Hibernica*; this they agreed to do. This distracted Nathaniel from his own project. More had left money in his will (he died in 1895) to assist with the republication. The second edition of *Cybele* was launched with a media splash in October 1898.[3]

Colgan restarted his Dublin project in the spring of 1899. He told none of his endeavours, he said, to avoid spending time on unsolicited material that he would have to double-check! Nathaniel's definitive survey, *Flora of the county Dublin*, was completed in September 1904 and published shortly thereafter. True to form, it was printed in Dublin and published by the Irish firm Hodges Figgis. It extended to seventy pages explaining how his survey was carried out, plus 324 pages of

detailed results. Colgan dedicated his book to Alexander Goodman
More, 'the foremost inspirer and guide of botanical research in
Ireland'. Over a century later, a scanned copy of the New York Public
Library's original edition was reprinted about the year 2010, by Nabu
Public Domain Reprints, because of the book's cultural importance.[4]

In 1955, the seventieth anniversary of the foundation of the Dublin
Naturalists' Field Club, a spokesperson expressed the hope of shortly
publishing a revised edition of *Flora of the county Dublin*.[5] It did not
happen shortly. In 1961 the National Museum published a ninety-
five-page supplement to Nathaniel's work.[6] To mark the centenary
of the setting up of the club, which would occur in 1986, the club
decided to repeat the flora survey that Nathaniel Colgan undertook
over the same eight districts. Fieldwork began in earnest in 1983 and
continued into the early 1990s. This was led by Declan Doogue, the
project's progress-chaser too, and he along with Messrs Nash, Parnell,
Reynolds and Wyse Jackson compiled and edited the end product,
an extraordinarily comprehensive tome of 558 pages, including 99
pages of prefatory content. This core group was assisted by fourteen
named contributors and by a total of forty-nine persons recording
specimens. The new book, *Flora of County Dublin*, was priced at £25
and took fifteen years to bring to fruition in the autumn of 1998, the
same duration it took Nathaniel Colgan to produce its predecessor.

5. Politics, nationalism and the secret police file

At one time, for whom one voted was not secret. The voting records show that Nathaniel's father, Nathaniel Watson Colgan, in the election of May 1859, voted for John Vance and Sir Edward Grogan.[1] Vance was a professional Conservative MP, an Orange man who opposed the Maynooth grant, and who coined the phrase 'Home Rule is Rome Rule'. Grogan was a Conservative Irish MP, educated in England and in TCD; he was a barrister. The Grogan lawyer family of north Kildare may be related to him. The *City of Dublin election, July 15th 1865 – the list of electors* (1865) includes a record for whom they voted. Nathaniel's father was by now dead, but his grandfather, Joseph Colgan, of 17 Brabazon Row, St Luke's parish, and then aged 73, voted for Vance and for Benjamin L. Guinness, both Unionists.

As a senior public official in a sensitive post, it would have been very imprudent for Nathaniel Colgan to disclose his political disposition; that did not prevent him being a fervent nationalist, from a cultural perspective. As well as joining *Conradh na Gaeilge*, a widely reported incident at the annual general meeting of the Dublin Naturalists' Field Club held at the RIA in 1914 is remarkable. After being elected president of the club for the coming year, Colgan protested against the use of the name 'London pride' for the Irish form of the plant named 'St Patrick's Cabbage'; he added that 'London pride' was, in any case, a mere corruption of 'London's pride', the garden plant having been originally so called after a horticulturalist by the name of London, who introduced it to notice.[2]

After Colgan's retirement as chief court clerk in 1916, secret government files reveal the disposition of the chief commissioner of police, which did not reflect favourably on Colgan (fig. 6). In January 1917, the commissioner wrote a letter marked 'Secret' to the undersecretary of state for Ireland about Mr T.V. Cleary, the senior second-class clerk at the Dublin Metropolitan Police courts and next

6a–b. Chief commissioner of police's secret files

in turn for promotion to the vacant first-class clerkship 'consequent on the retirement of Mr Nathaniel Colgan, late chief clerk'. The writer objected to Cleary's promotion (and, indeed, his employment at all), for he was an Irish Volunteer and involved in the Gaelic League, and a house search found a Martini Henry rifle there converted to .22 ammunition. 'I believe Mr Nathaniel Colgan, late chief clerk, exerted strong influence to shield Mr Cleary'.[3] Mr Cleary did not get the job.

While there was unfavourable evaluations of Colgan recorded on secret police files, he, nevertheless, pledged £2 a month for six months to provide food for the members of the Royal Dublin Fusiliers who were prisoners of the enemy in the First World War, which was then ongoing.[4] His nephew, George Colgan, Revd William's younger son, served in France until he was reported killed in action in April 1919.

The political, cultural and religious disposition of persons and families can sometimes be gleaned from what they do with their discretionary funds. Little is known of the charitable disposition of

Nathaniel Colgan's father, and nothing of his female ancestors. And only a small number of charitable donations ever reached the printed media. However, when a petition was signed by over 80,000 people from all parts of Ireland and England, aimed at securing clemency from the death sentence passed on William Smith O'Brien, the leader of a failed rebellion that took place in 1848, it included thirty Colgans in Ireland. Among those signing were the pawnbroker, Nathaniel Watson Colgan (the naturalist's father); his silk-weaver father, Joseph Colgan, and his brother, another Joseph, from Bishop Street – whom I believe to be another pawnbroker's apprentice. The following year, 1849, a letter to the editor of the *Freeman's Journal* from 'the pawnbrokers' assistants of Dublin' on alleviating 'the extreme distress prevailing among their less fortunate fellow-countrymen of the west and south', stated that they had raised the sum of £24 4s. 6d. Among those who contributed were Nathaniel Watson Colgan (10s.) and his brother Joseph (5s.).[5] Shortly after the death of Nathaniel Watson Colgan, his representatives gave £2 to the central committee for relief of distress in Ireland – I presume this to be a prior commitment by Colgan.[6] The earliest, published, charitable contribution believed to be from Nathaniel Colgan (the younger) of £1 to a special coal fund (on the north side of Dublin) for the benefit of the poor, without religious discrimination, was paid about New Year 1894, when he was aged 42. The largest contributions were from Lord Iveagh, Messrs Arthur Guinness and the lord lieutenant, each of whom paid £10.[7] Details were published in 1897 of contributors to the Queen's Diamond Jubilee Commemoration Fund; the monies raised were used to finance the Queen Victoria Jubilee Institute of Nurses (more commonly known as Jubilee Nurses), who provided care and assistance to the Irish sick poor in their own homes: Lord Iveagh contributed the largest amount by far, £12,500; the lord lieutenant, £500; Nathaniel Colgan gave £1.[8]

In 1904 the Mansion House Coal Fund was set up to alleviate the awful hardship of the poor in Dublin city. The Dublin Tobacconists' Association sent a cheque for £3 3s. Two managers of the National Bank sent a cheque for £9 1s., being their own and the bank staff's contributions. Nathaniel Colgan sent a cheque for £3, being from the clerical staff of the police courts of which he was the chief clerk. The Rt Hon. Justice Barton donated £5 5s.; and there were several smaller donations.[9]

7. 15 Breffni Terrace, overlooking Bullock Harbour, Sandycove Road,
Glasthule, May 2013

Most instances of charitable donations go unrecorded. There are
some exceptions – donations of exemplars of botanical and marine
life that Colgan collected during his sojourns into the countryside and
to the seaside. It is suffice to reference several newspaper and official
reports here.[10]

6. Living quarters, retirement and death

Until he was nearly 30 years of age (1880), Nathaniel lived at Rehoboth House, Dolphin's Barn, SCR, Dublin. He was then still a junior clerk in the Dublin police court, based in the King's Inns. By 1888 he had moved with his family and resided at 1 Belgrave Road, Rathmines. By 1894, Slater's *Royal national directory of Ireland* states that he was living in Kingstown, now known as Dun Laoghaire. Perhaps he was. This would include his residence at 15 Breffni Terrace, Sandycove, Kingstown (fig. 7). However, he was still living with his older, deaf brother, John Joseph, and his sisters, Nannie, Letitia and Sarah, at 1 Belgrave Road, Rathmines, as recently as 1898. Sarah died at this address of tuberculosis at the age of 37 on 31 May 1898.[1] By 1900 the surviving siblings had moved to 15 Breffni Terrace, on Breffni Road, overlooking Bullock Harbour at Glasthule, Co. Dublin. This was an imposing three-storey-over-basement house of nine rooms, set back from the road with extensive gardens front and rear and well appointed. During the mid-1880s, the houses on this terrace were described as 'new' and recent advertisements state they were built in 1860. Number 15 was not sold to Nathaniel at any time close to his moving in about 1900, so one presumes either he bought it years earlier and rented it out until he needed it for his own use, or he rented it from a landlord for the remainder of his life. These houses, close by the sea, were in demand as holiday or permanent homes (with a rental value of around £65 a year at this time, 1893), and enjoyed, 'certified sewage and hot and cold bath' as the adverts for renting stated. The main bedroom, on the second floor, ran the full width of the house and overlooked Bullock Harbour. There the surviving siblings resided, along with a servant, until John J., Nannie and Nathaniel died, whereafter Letitia – Nathaniel's heir – or the landlord, sold it by auction in April 1920. This was not long after the death of the eldest sibling, John Joseph, in 1920.

Advert: Auction on Thursday next of semi-detached residence, 15 Breffni Terrace, Sandycove, with clear possession, containing 9 apartments, hot and cold bath, large garden front and rere. James Allen & Son, Auctioneers and Valuers, 53 Sackville Street, Dublin.[2]

15 Breffni Terrace was to be Nathaniel's last home. He retired at the end of 1916. He had contracted bladder cancer in 1917 or perhaps had an earlier warning of it. He cut back on his lectures and other commitments. At the end of April 1919 a paper due to be read by him to the Royal Irish Academy was read in his stead by Prof. Augustine Henry.[3] His second nephew, George, had been reported as having been killed in action that week.

Nathaniel died at home on Thursday 2 October 1919, with his brother, the Revd William Henry Colgan, attending to him.[4] Nathaniel was 68. He is said to have had a large collection of around 2,000 plants in his Breffni Terrace garden. In his will dated 6 April 1916 – the first day of the tax year – Nathaniel appointed his sister, Letitia, as his executor and the sole beneficiary of his estate, which she declared was worth £4,832-odd, equivalent to €360,500 in 2022 money.[5]

We know that Nathaniel took an interest in religion and philosophy as a young man of 22, when he wrote an article on Sir Thomas Browne, a physician and author of the bestseller *Religio Medici* (1643), a spiritual and psychological self-assessment; and the following year (1874) an article on the writer, physician, anti-clerical free-thinker, François Rabelais (1493–1553). His botanizing and mountaineering friend, Bishop D'Arcy, wrote of him that he was not enamoured of organized religion and less so of the Catholic religious orders. There is an indication that Nathaniel had taken a bit more kindly to the Church – for which he had little time, and jaundiced views on, but no overt hostility, for most of his life: at the age of 37 he had been elected as sidesman to Sandford church, near Marlborough Road, at Easter 1888.[6] This may have been as a gesture to his brother, William, who had recently been ordained a priest in the Church of Ireland.

It was from his Glasthule home that Nathaniel had begun to take an interest in marine life – Bullock Harbour and other seaside places being near at hand. Contemporaries speculated that he did so simply to change from botany after he had published his *Flora of the County Dublin* (1904) and also because he lived near the sea now. His friend Robin [Robert] Praeger provided a list of his publications (apart from those published in the journal itself), in the *Irish Naturalist*.[7]

Colgan was interred in the family plot at Mount Jerome, Dublin, alongside his grandfather, Joseph, his parents and the siblings who came before and after him, his brother, Revd William Henry Colgan, excepted. The latter died on 15 June 1942, at Forfey House, Lisnaskea, Co. Fermanagh, where he had served as rector. He is said to be buried there; I could find no trace of his grave in the churchyard. Forfey House is in ruins. As might be expected of a scrupulous researcher, Nathaniel had copious details inscribed on his own headstone. Gravestone no. 13082 in Mount Jerome Cemetery, Dublin, reads:

> In memory of Joseph Colgan who died 27/11/1878 aged 86 years – Of his son Nathaniel (Watson) died 23/1/1863 aged 44 years – of Letitia wife of Nathaniel died 26/4/1865 aged 38 years – And of their children – Joseph died 5/10/1861 aged 4 years – Elizabeth died 6/10/1861 aged 6 years – Joseph died 1/3/1864 aged 1 year – Sarah died 31/5/1898 aged 37 years – Nannie died 23/1/1916 aged 68 years – Nathaniel, second son of Nathaniel Colgan died 2/10/1919 aged 68 years – John Joseph, eldest son of Nathaniel, died 27/1/1920 aged 70 years – Interred in Grant, 15729

The last surviving sister, Letitia, by now aged 67, moved to live with her nephew, Dr John Colgan, the surviving son of her youngest brother, Revd William Henry, at Oakdene, Fleetwood, Lancashire, where he worked for the council as a medical officer. William, it should be noted, was the only one of his siblings to marry and Dr John (Jack) was the only surviving male from the next generation. Two years later to the month since moving to England, there appeared the following death notice:

> COLGAN: April 18 1922, at 2 Warren Avenue, Oak Dene, Fleetwood, Lancashire, Letitia Colgan, daughter of late Nathaniel Colgan, of Dublin, sister of Revd William Colgan, Ballinlough, Roscommon.[8]

Letitia Colgan appointed her brother, Revd William, and her nephew, Dr John, as her executors and she left a personal estate of £6,372-odd, most of which was in Ireland. She left small bequests to her two nieces, Mrs Mary Constance Cameron and Mrs Hilda Clarke; larger bequests to her two first cousins, daughters of her mother's sister (Angelica Phair): Angelica and Annie Hunter; and the smallest bequest, to Dr John's wife, Harriet Elizabeth Colgan. To her brother, William, she left an annuity of £100 for the rest of his expected life and the remainder of her estate to Dr John Colgan.[9]

7. Tributes

The *Irish Times* published an anonymous obituary on 6 October 1919. It stated, *inter alia*, that after joining the staff of the Dublin police court, Nathaniel Colgan served there for forty years, and retired about three years ago under the age limit when chief clerk. His intimate knowledge of the law and processes of his office made him a valuable officer and trustworthy adviser to all who consulted him ... He had a genial manner ... and enjoyed the friendship of the magistrates.

He was a close friend of the renowned naturalist, Alexander Goodman More. In conjunction with Dr Reginald Scully of Kerry Colgan produced a second edition of the *Cybele Hibernica*. The first edition was published in 1866; the authors were David Moore and Alexander More, who More died in 1895. More's sister was a neighbour of the Colgans in Rathmines and provided Nathaniel and Scully with the funding, out of Alexander's estate, to publish the second edition.[1] More had encouraged both Colgan and Scully to compile their inventories of flora in counties Dublin and Kerry, respectively. Nathaniel left behind a most valuable collection of plants. He received a well-deserved honour of election to the Royal Irish Academy – More was one of his nominators – and was president of the Dublin Naturalists' Field Club. He had a wonderful facility for languages, German, French, Danish, Norwegian and Swedish, and he was a first-rate Irish scholar. He corresponded even with Japanese naturalists.[2] Of the revised edition of *Cybele Hibernica*, the *Freeman's Journal* remarked (1898):

> Botanists had been waiting impatiently for an up-to-date record of the distribution of flowering plants in Ireland. The first edition of this was published in 1866 by David Moore and A.G. More, in collaboration. In 1895 More died, leaving funds to his two friends, Nathaniel Colgan and Reginald Scully to complete and publish the work. The first-edition material is still there, but

is more complete. In this listing the publications of the Royal Irish Academy, the Royal Dublin Society and the *Journal of Botany* are frequently quoted.[3]

During his time residing at Rehoboth House – a house built originally to accommodate a couple and their twenty-four children who survived to adulthood – Nathaniel befriended another resident, Charles Frederick D'Arcy, whose family was from Westmeath. D'Arcy's grandfather, Brierly, had a lease on the house. D'Arcy was a contemporary of Nathaniel's brother, William, and both studied at Trinity College Dublin at about the same time. Charles and Nathaniel became friends and went climbing mountains along with William. Here is what Charles (archbishop of Armagh at his death in 1938) wrote in his biography: 'As a young man we made several fine ascents in the Alps and he had climbed in every mountain range in Ireland'. D'Arcy wrote that his friendship with the two Colgan brothers was based on their all being lovers of the wild: 'to get away, anywhere, out of the grimy grubby city, to mountain, moor or forest – that was our delight'. Nathaniel, he wrote, 'was a climber of rare ability'. 'He suffered from an excess of modesty' but 'it did not rob his conversation of a gentle and delicious irony which played over the surface of every theme'. D'Arcy wrote that 'the manners and methods of the churches did not attract him (Nathaniel)'. Of the Roman Catholic religious orders he – Nathaniel – declared, casually, 'These people would like to have us all under lock and key'. 'My friend was filled with a passion for freedom. For this reason, he abhorred socialism in all its forms'.

In a short obituary on D'Arcy's death, it is stated that 'Many of the discoveries in Nathaniel Colgan's *Cybele Hibernica* were made in the presence of that friend of his college days'.[4] Nathaniel was not in college; it was his younger brother, William, who was in Trinity with D'Arcy.

Robert Lloyd Praeger (1865–1953) was a native of Hollywood, Co. Down; an engineer by profession, he worked as a librarian in the National Library of Ireland from 1893 to 1923. He was a naturalist by inclination and rose to become president of the Royal Irish Academy. He probably met Nathaniel in the National Library of Ireland. Of Nathaniel, he wrote in his obituary[5] that Colgan developed an interest in natural history comparatively late in life, unequipped with a scientific training, and diffident about seeking information from fellow-workers. He nevertheless found himself – almost against his will – drawn into the scientific life of Dublin. Courteous, humorous and a real lover of nature, he earned the friendship and respect of a large body of Irish naturalists, and his death will be deplored widely. ... In 1875 he had undertaken the first of a series of summer tours which added greatly to the interest of life ... On many of these trips he had pleasant and useful companions, whose comradeship ripened into life-long friendships. ... France, Italy, Switzerland, Spain and Morocco were visited in turn ... [as well] as the west of Ireland.

Praeger quotes an anonymous source: 'He loved his country and helped to know it and make it known in his own quiet way: he loved true knowledge and followed its beck along many paths. His contribution to humanity, knowledge and culture is a real one, and worthy of imitation'.

* * *

Nathaniel Colgan's main claim to fame is that he managed over a long period, with the occasional assistance of two sisters and his younger brother, to track down and record all the wild plants of every kind in the whole county of Dublin. He did it without the aid of the internet, the motor car or the mobile telephone and essentially on his own. And he did it without any formal third-level education in the field, other than what he gleaned in a kind of apprenticeship with friends in academia. To their credit, his academic peers in the Royal Irish Academy acknowledged his talent with full membership. That the same exercise was repeated nearly a century later, but with a team of a dozen or more under the guidance of Dr Declan Doogue, and in the same overall time, is testimony to both the importance of Colgan's research and his capacity to work on his own. We know that he avoided publicity about it so that he could avoid having to check unsolicited samples proffered by well-wishers. With the public,

Colgan would be best known for his quirky, populist study of the 'true' shamrock, which showed he had a flair for self-publicity, hardly the mark of a shy person. He partook of singing to entertain, and showing slides of his travels with his pal, the Church of Ireland archbishop of Dublin, a classmate of his brother, the priest, William Colgan. Few noticed his significant interest in the Irish language and music and only a rare one would have known of his advocacy of a rebel candidate for his job on retirement. This candidate was a member of the Volunteers and was found with a Martini rifle in his home.

Little was known of his early life until now, for he and his siblings were orphaned at an early age. His surviving sisters, and a deaf older brother, lived with Nathaniel in his home and all remained unmarried with one exception. His several life interests: botany, mountaineering, court work, and the promotion of Irish language and culture, were compartmentalised among his acquaintances and friends. Memories only of his botany, and to a lesser extent, his mountaineering, have survived. The early deaths, after his own, of siblings living with him, departures to England of a sister and his surviving nephew and other family happenstance left few, if any, to sustain his memory. If only the dna of a male descendant were to hand, one could go deeper into his family's past. Nathaniel Colgan was undoubtedly a nerd, but one who was full of the joys of spring.

Appendix

A representative selection of Nathaniel Colgan's publications

'Sir Thomas Browne and the *Religio Medici* (1643)', *Varieties* (1873).

'François Rabelais (1493–1553)', *Varieties* (1874).

'A translation from Richter', *Irish Monthly*, 7 (1879), pp 24–30.

'Netherland Genre Pictures', *Irish Monthly*, 7 (1879), pp 628–34.

'Up and round Mont Blanc', *Irish Monthly*, 8:79–83 (1880), in four parts.

'A bull-fight at Granada in 1880', *Irish Monthly*, 9:99 (1881), pp 491–8.

'The shamrock: an attempt to fix its species', *Irish Naturalist*, 1:5 (Aug. 1892), pp 95–7.

'*Speculara Hybrida* in Co. Dublin', *Irish Naturalist*, 1:7 (Oct. 1892), pp 144–5.

'Notes on the flora of the Aran Islands', *Irish Naturalist*, 3:4 (Apr. 1893), pp 106–11.

'The shamrock: a further attempt to fix its species', *Irish Naturalist*, 2:8 (Aug. 1893), pp 202–11.

'Notes on the flora of Co. Dublin', *Irish Naturalist*, 2:11 (Oct. 1893), pp 283–8.

'Henry Mundy and the shamrock', *Journal of Botany* (1894), pp 109–11.

'Witchcraft in the Aran Islands', *Journal of the Royal Society of Antiquaries of Ireland*, 5:1 (Mar. 1895), pp 84–5.

'The shamrock in literature', *Journal of the Royal Society of Antiquaries of Ireland*, 26 (1896), pp 211–26, 349–61.

With Reginald W. Scully, 2nd ed. of Alexander G. More's *Contributions towards a* Cybele Hibernica (1898).

'Remarks on the second edition of *Cybele Hibernica*: a rejoinder', *Irish Naturalist*, 9:3 (Mar. 1900), pp 56–8: with Reginald Scully.

'Notes on Irish topographical botany, with some remarks on floral diversity', *Irish Naturalist*, 10:12 (Dec. 1901), pp 233–40.

'Is the frog a native of Ireland?', *Irish Naturalist*, 13:4 (Jan. 1904), pp 93–4.

Flora of the county Dublin (1904).

'Sagacity of the herring gull', *Irish Naturalist*, 15:1 (Jan. 1906), pp 14–16.

'The scientific tourist through Ireland', *Irish Naturalist*, 15:11 (Nov. 1906), pp 252–3: with Richard M. Barrington and R. Lloyd Praeger.

'The ship-worm and wood-boring crustaceans in Kingstown Harbour', *Irish Naturalist*, 17:1 (Jan. 1908), pp 9–14.

'Dublin Marine Biological Committee: general account of dredging operations 1907, with special notes on the mollusca', *Irish Naturalist*, 17:6 (June 1908), pp 105–14.

'An Irish naturalist in Spain in the eighteenth century', *Irish Naturalist*, 20:1 (Jan. 1911), pp 1–5.

'Clare Island Survey: Gaelic plant and animal names and associated folk-lore', *Proceedings of the Royal Irish Academy*, 31:4 (1911), pp 1–30.

'On Irish animal names', *Irish Naturalist*, 24:9 (Sept. 1915), pp 166–9.

'Lusitania and Kerry: a botanical parallel', *Irish Naturalist*, 27:2 (Feb. 1918), pp 22–6.

'On the reproduction of the common garden snail, *Helix Aspersa*', *Irish Naturalist*, 27:12 (Dec. 1918), pp 165–70.

'On the occurrence of tropical drift seeds on the Irish Atlantic coasts', *Proceedings of the Royal Irish Academy*, 35 (1919–20), pp 29–54.

Notes

AGM	Annual General Meeting
b.	born
d.	died
DNA	deoxyribonucleic acid
FTCD	Fellow of Trinity College Dublin
GRO	General Register's Office
HOC	House of Commons
JRSAI	*Journal of the Royal Society of Antiquaries of Ireland*
MRIA	Member of the Royal Irish Academy
NAI	National Archives of Ireland
NUI	National University of Ireland
PRIA	*Proceedings of the Royal Irish Academy*
RIA	Royal Irish Academy
SCR	South Circular Road
s.p.	single person
TCD	Trinity College Dublin

1. A TRAGIC EARLY LIFE

1 *Freeman's Journal*, 7 Oct. 1861, 8 Oct. 1861; *Cork Examiner*, 9 Oct. 1861.

2 St Andrew's Parish Register and GRO, 5, p. 189, Q1, 1846, Dublin South.

3 William Smith-O'Brien petition, 1848–9; Griffith's Valuation, *c.*1850.

4 Smith-O'Brien petition, 1848–9.

5 *Freeman's Journal*, 24 Jan. 1863; *Cork Examiner*, 26 Jan. 1863.

6 *Irish Times*, 31 May 1862.

7 *Registry of Deeds*, 1861-22-46.

8 Wills and Administrations, 1863, NAI, no. 69; *Index to Irish administrations, 1863*; folio no. 87 or 89; NAI.

9 *Freeman's Journal*, 24 Apr. 1862.

10 The birth date, 28 May 1851, for Nathaniel Colgan is from his friend, R. Lloyd Praeger's obituary for Nathaniel Colgan in *The Irish Naturalist*, Nov.–Dec. 1919, p. 121. This date is reconcilable with Nathaniel's declared age in two censuses. Christenings of Nathaniel and his siblings have been neither confirmed nor located.

11 GRO, p. 224, Q4, no. 350, 1889, Galway, no. 2.

12 Joseph Colgan died in the Old Men's Asylum, Rathmines: GRO, p. 510, Q4, 1878, Dublin South.

13 Mount Jerome, Gravestone Number 13082.

14 Veronica Rowe, www.weavespindye.ie/history (last accessed 7 Apr. 2022).

15 As the voluntary administrator of the Colgan surname project with the earliest and largest agency for DNA testing for genealogical purposes in the world, FamilyTreeDNA.com, I have taken a special interest in this aspect of Nathaniel Colgan's genealogy.

16 'Priestfield', beside Rehoboth House, advertised for sale in 1815: *Freeman's Journal*, 19 May 1815.

17 *Freeman's Journal*, 28 Apr. 1865.

18 Dublin City Census, 1851.

19 seamuscullen.net (accessed 1 Oct. 2019).

20 *Irish Independent*, 7 Mar. 1912; *Freeman's Journal*, 21 June 1912.

21 English GRO, p. 1034, V8e, Q2, 1922, Fylde District.

22 English GRO, p. 274, V100, Q2, 1959, Fylde District.

2. SCHOOLING AND THE DAY JOB

1 *Irish Independent*, 7 Mar. 1912.
2 *Freeman's Journal*, 3 June 1869.
3 *Saunders's News-Letter*, 3 Apr. 1871.
4 *Irish Times*, 4 Apr., 20 May 1871; *Saunders's News-Letter*, 13 May 1871.
5 HOC Papers, 1871 (C445).
6 *Londonderry Standard*, 24 Feb. 1872; *Freeman's Journal*, 9 Mar. 1872.
7 *Irish Times*, 2 Jan. 1873.
8 *Freeman's Journal*, 16 Aug. 1856, 1 Jan. 1857; *Saunders's News-Letter*, 9 Feb. 1857, 26 Apr. 1858, 14 Mar. 1860; *Irish Times*, 14 Mar., 31 Mar. 1860; *Freeman's Journal*, 16 June 1860; *Irish Times*, 31 May 1862.
9 *Freeman's Journal*, 18 July 1912.
10 *Irish Times*, 12 Nov. 1938.
11 *Freeman's Journal*, 27 May 1872, 3 June 1873.
12 Charles F. D'Arcy, *The adventures of a bishop* (London, 1938), on Rehoboth House (pp 14, 15) and of his wanderings with the Colgan brothers and Doyle.
13 *The Times*, 2 Feb. 1938.
14 *Dublin Daily Express*, 9 Dec. 1891, 21 Mar. 1892; *Irish Times*, 14 Feb. 1907; *Freeman's Journal*, 14 Feb. 1912; *Dublin Daily Express*, 4, 11 Nov. 1914.
15 *Freeman's Journal*, 25 July 1912.

3. INTEREST IN IRISH LANGUAGE AND CULTURE

1 *Irish Times*, 8 Oct. 1919.
2 *Freeman's Journal*, 13 Mar. 1896.
3 *Irish Independent*, 25 May 1897.
4 *Dublin Daily Nation*, 29 Oct. 1897.
5 *Irish Independent*, 18 May 1899.
6 *Dublin Evening Telegraph*, 22 Oct. 1900; *Freeman's Journal*, 27 Feb. 1899.
7 *Irish Times*, 10 Apr. 1902.
8 *Irish Times*, 15 Apr. 1905; *Dublin Daily Express*, 20 Apr. 1905.
9 Written communication from Konstantin Ermolin, library assistant, RIA.
10 *Freeman's Journal*, 27, 28 Feb. 1911; *Dublin Daily Express*, 27 Feb. 1911.
11 *PRIA*, 31:4 (1911), pp 1–30.
12 *Dublin Daily Express*, 28 Feb. 1911.
13 *Freeman's Journal*, 14 Feb. 1914.
14 *Dublin Daily Express*, 12 Mar. 1914.
15 *Irish Times*, 23 Dec. 1904; *Weekly Irish Times*, 31 Dec. 1904.

16 Nathaniel's younger brother, William, also had a gift for languages – seven – and excelled in them in college – TCD – and put his Irish to use spreading the Protestant message in the Gaeltacht of Co. Galway: *Irish Times*, 12 Nov. 1938.
17 *Freeman's Journal*, p. 2, 27 Feb. 1899.
18 See Joe Kennedy, *Irish Independent*, 15 Mar. 2004.
19 Fortuitously, as a principal officer at the National Board for Science & Technology, I managed a grant scheme which awarded a grant to an NUI Maynooth professor for work on legumes and nitrogen fixation (*c*.1980).
20 *Westminster Gazette*, 18 Mar. 1920.
21 *Wicklow People*, 15 Oct. 1892; *Wexford People*, 15 Oct. 1892; *Enniscorthy Guardian*, 15 Oct. 1892; *Hull Daily Mail*, 30 Jan. 1893; *Nenagh Guardian*, 1 Feb. 1893; *Freeman's Journal*, 2 Feb. 1893.
22 *Daily Telegraph*, 27 Jan. 1893; *The Field*, 28 Jan. 1893.
23 *London Daily News*, 6 Jan. 1893.
24 Nathaniel Colgan, 'Henry Mundy and the Shamrock' in *Journal of Botany* (1894), pp 109–11.
25 *JRSAI*, 26:3 (Sept. 1896), pp 211–26; *JRSAI*, 26:4 (Dec. 1896), pp 349–61.
26 *The Times*, 17 Mar. 1914.
27 *JRSAI*, 24:2 (June 1894), pp 132–5.
28 *Irish Times, Dublin Evening Mail*, 17 Mar. 1896.
29 *Irish Times, Freeman's Journal, Dublin Daily Express*, 16 Mar. 1910.
30 *Irish Times, Dublin Daily Express*, 17 Mar. 1911.
31 *Irish Times*, 17 Mar. 1926.
32 Edward Colgan, *For want of good money: the story of Ireland's coinage* (Bray, 2003).

4. MAGNUM OPUS: *FLORA OF THE COUNTY DUBLIN*

1 Letitia, cited on pp 157 (Vesey's Lucan Demesne, 1904), 197 (Howth, 1903); Sarah on pp 2 (Malahide, 1897), 114 (Sutton, 1896), 120 (Howth, 1896), 163 (Howth, 1897), 193 (Malahide, 1897), 196 (ditto), 290 (Howth, 1896); Miss Colgan on pp 18 (Kingstown pier, 1904), 112 (Dalkey quarry, 1904); Revd William on pp ix, xxx, 156, 165, 182.

2 *Freeman's Journal*, 15 Mar. 1895; *Belfast News-Letter*, 9 July 1903, 10 Mar. 1904.
3 *The Times*, 20 Oct. 1898; *Dublin Daily Express*, 22 Oct. 1898.
4 The book does not include an index of place-names; I have, however, compiled details of pages referring to Leixlip, Salmon Leap and St Catherine's: Leixlip: pp xxxii, lix, lxii, 4, 8, 43, 75, 92, 94, 98, 122, 123, 156, 161, 210, 234; Salmon Leap: xxi, 8, 43, 92, 148, 177, 209, 210, 224, 265, 268; St Catherine's: lx, 35, 43, 123, 148, 151, 155, 156, 157, 164, 186, 242, 283.
5 *Irish Times*, 2 Sept. 1955.
6 *Irish Times*, 30 Mar. 1960, 26 Apr., 3 May 1986.

5. POLITICS, NATIONALISM AND THE SECRET POLICE FILE
1 List of electors, city of Dublin election, May 1859.
2 *Freeman's Journal, Irish Times, Dublin Daily Express*, 23 Jan. 1914.
3 Colonial Office Records, Dublin Castle Special Branch Files, CO904/196/57.
4 *Irish Times*, 5 Dec. 1916; *Freeman's Journal*, 5 Dec. 1916.
5 *Freeman's Journal*, 30 May 1849.
6 *Freeman's Journal*, 20 Feb. 1863.

7 *Irish Times*, 16 Jan. 1894.
8 *Dublin Daily Express*, 1 May 1897.
9 *Irish Independent*, 28 Nov. 1904.
10 *Dublin Evening Mail*, 17 Mar. 1896; HOC Papers, 1896 (Cd. 7941); HOC Papers, 1901 (Cd. 113); 1902 (Cd. 1314); 1908 (Cd. 4148); 1908 (Cd. 4430); 1911 (Cd. 5611); 1914 (Cd. 7298); *Irish Times*, 29 Apr. 1919.

6. LIVING QUARTERS, RETIREMENT AND DEATH
1 GRO, p. 500, Q2, 1898, Rathmines, Dublin South.
2 *Irish Independent*, 12 Apr. 1920.
3 *Freeman's Journal*, 29 Apr. 1919.
4 GRO, p. 619, Q4, 1919, Kingstown, no. 2, Rathdrum.
5 Testamentary Records, NAI.
6 *Dublin Daily Express*, 5 Apr. 1888.
7 *Irish Naturalist*, Nov.–Dec. 1919, pp 121–6.
8 *Irish Times*, 29 Apr. 1922.
9 NAI, Testamentary Records.

7. TRIBUTES
1 *Weekly Irish Times*, 11 May 1935; *Irish Times*, 11 Feb. 1909.
2 *Irish Times*, 8 Oct. 1919.
3 *Freeman's Journal*, 3 Nov. 1898.
4 *The Times*, 2 Feb. 1938.
5 *Irish Naturalist*, Nov.–Dec. 1919.